Introduct

C000184273

The first guide to **Walks on the Clv**
very popular with local people a
routes based upon Offa's Dyke Path, g
side of the designated Area of Outstan
ond book, free from such constraints, explores the many other beautiful parts of the Clwydian Range and adjoining countryside, including
The Loggerheads and *Moel Famau Country Parks*. In particular, it cov-
ers in depth the large area of carboniferous limestone which forms
such a significant, yet perhaps less well known, part of the Range,
including several Sites of Special Scientific Interest. Formed millions
of years ago when North Wales was covered by a tropical sea, and
later tilted by major earth movements, the exposed limestone escarpments, pavements, and outcrops, provide stunning scenery which
contrasts with the lush green hills and valleys, and offers such
delightful walking. The area from Hendre to Llananarmon-y-Ial contained rich seams of lead within the underlying limestone, and was
extensively mined between the 17th and 19th centuries.

This industrial heritage is a backcloth to many of the walks, which
explore open hills, attractive woodland, the undulating countryside
overlooking the coast, and include the beautiful wooded Alyn Valley
with its famous 'leete path', impressive limestone escarpments, and
the network of old miners paths. They visit iron-age hill forts,
medieval sites, ancient communities, lead-mining villages, nature
reserves, and old country inns.

The routes, which range between 5 – 8 miles, follow public rights
of way or permissive paths, and are well within the capability of most
walkers. Many routes contain shorter walk options, *and a key feature
is that individual walks can easily be linked with others, to provide
longer and more challenging day routes if required*. Walking boots or
strong shoes are recommended, along with appropriate clothing to
protect against the elements. *And please remember that the condition
of the paths can vary according to season and weather!*

Each walk has a detailed map and description which enables the
route to be followed without difficulty, but be aware that changes can
occur at any time. The location of each walk is shown on the back
cover and a summary of their key characteristics is also provided. This
includes an estimated walking time, but the scenery is far too good to
hurry through, so allow more time for its enjoyment. Most walks are
accessible by public transport – details can be obtained by calling
01824 706968. Please observe the country code.

Enjoy your walking!

WALK 1
GOLDEN GROVE AND SEA VIEWS

DESCRIPTION An exhilarating 6¼ mile walk with breathtaking contrasting views of coast, sea, estuary, towns, hills and mountains from the most northerly section of the Clwydian Hills. The route links two ancient and attractive settlements, both with characterful country inns, and passes a 16thC mansion. It includes a section of Offa's Dyke Path along the steep west-facing Prestatyn Hillside – a Site of Special Scientific Interest – offering commanding views, which compensate for the subsequent effort to regain height. Allow about 3½ hours. The amount of uphill walking can be reduced by going directly to points **3** or **4**. The route can also be undertaken as two shorter walks. Binoculars are recommended.

START Gwaenysgor [SJ 075811] or alternatively Llanasa [SJ 106815].

DIRECTIONS Gwaenysgor is signposted from the A5151 just west of Trelawnyd. Roadside parking is available in the village centre. (For information on Gwaenysgor see **Walk 2**). Llanasa is signposted from the centre of Trelawnyd. A car park is available opposite the parish church.

1 Head north through the village and, after about 100 yards, turn half-LEFT past Brynffynon, dated 1680, soon along an enclosed path to reach the village well – *the main source of water until after the First World War*. Continue along the path, over a stile, to soon reach the open gorse-covered hillside, before crossing a stile ahead at a stunning viewpoint. *Here you look over the Clwyd delta to the vast expanse of the coast stretching to the Great Orme, and the mountains of Snowdonia beyond. To the south lie the central Clwydian Hills.*

2 Turn RIGHT to enjoy an exhilarating section of the Offa's Dyke Path along the edge of Prestatyn Hillside, before gradually descending past a quarry to a road. Follow it

to the RIGHT, then, after about 200 yards, turn sharp RIGHT on a rising path, after passing toilets. Just beyond the first steps, go half-LEFT and on up a stepped path through small conifers, before heading half-RIGHT to a waymark post by *Tyn yr Allt*. Continue up by the edge of a wood, then turn LEFT down a road.

3 At the bend, go RIGHT to follow a path alongside the wood edge and cross a stile into a field. Follow the boundary on the left for 20 yards to cross a stile. Head half-RIGHT up the field to cross a stile in the corner, and continue half-LEFT to cross a stile ahead. Now go slightly RIGHT to cross another stile ahead, then walk half-LEFT across the next field to reach a track.

4 Follow the track LEFT, soon swinging RIGHT by a Police radio mast. *Ahead are far-reaching views across the mouth of the Dee Estuary to the distant Lancashire coast.* When the track swings down left by a ruined house, turn RIGHT to follow a delightful enclosed bridleway rising along the edge of the replanted Acre Wood, before contouring along the hillside. *On a clear day the Lake*

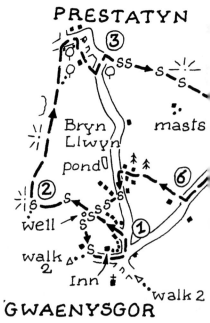

PRESTATYN

Bryn Llwyn

masts

pond

well

walk 2

Inn

walk 2

GWAENYSGOR

2

District mountains and Blackpool Tower can be seen. *Prominent on the shoreline is the former Talacre lighthouse.* After passing a house, continue along its access track. *Out at sea you will see a gas-drilling platform and many ships, including the regular ferry passing between Ireland and Liverpool.* At another bridleway, swing RIGHT with the track to an excellent viewpoint. *From here you can survey the length of the Dee estuary, the Wirral peninsular, and the Liverpool skyline beyond, with its cathedrals clearly visible. The character of the estuary changes significantly according to the tides – from a vast expanse of water to exposed sandbanks!* Continue to the road at Llanasa. Turn RIGHT, soon passing the 17thC Henblas Hall to reach the Red Lion, where refreshments are available.

L lanasa, with its pristine stone buildings, was founded around the church of the second Bishop of St. Asaph. The church's east window is said to have come from Basingwerk Abbey upon its dissolution in the 16thC. In the graveyard are buried many people who have drowned in the nearby Dee estuary, including the crew of the Point of Air lifeboat who drowned on 4th January 1854 in heavy seas. Following this tragedy, crew were instructed to wear the new cork lifejackets, or risk a fine.

stile ahead. Continue in the same direction. *Down to your left is Golden Grove – a stylish 16thC mansion originally the seat of the Morgan family.* Cross two stiles in the field corner by a small pond. Turn RIGHT after the pond, then swing sharp LEFT across the undulating field alongside telegraph posts to cross two stiles at the top edge of a plantation. Continue alongside the wood edge to cross a stile by St. Elmo's wood, which was planted in 1994. *It takes its name from a summerhouse which once graced the top of the hillside, on a site also used by the Morgans as a pet's graveyard.* Now head towards the masts to reach the track by your outward route.

6 Follow it to the LEFT. It soon drops steadily down and becomes a lane. Turn RIGHT along a waymarked enclosed bridleway to reach a road by Bryn Llwyn pond – *a haven for coots and moorhens.* Follow the road LEFT and shortly cross a stile on the right. Follow the waymarked path across two fields to reach the well. *If you took an alternative outward route, I recommend that you divert right the short distance to enjoy the superb viewpoint at point 2.* Cross the stone

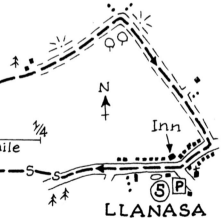

5 Take the road signposted to Gwaenysgor/ Trelawnyd, passing the old village pump by a pond, to leave Llanasa. Just before a small wood, cross a stile on the right. Head half-LEFT up through three fields to cross a stile in the top corner by a small plantation. Go up its edge, over another stile, then go half-LEFT across the next field to cross a

stile opposite. Keep along the field edge, cross a ladder-stile, then swing LEFT to cross another stile and on to a track. Follow it LEFT to join a lane for a rewarding finish at the Eagle and Child inn.

3

WALK 2
GOP HILL AND MARIAN MILL

DESCRIPTION A fascinating 6 mile walk exploring the undulating countryside around Trelawnyd and associated places of historical interest, with excellent views. Highlights include an easy climb to the ancient summit cairn on Gop Hill – the largest in Wales, a visit to the old settlement of Gwaenysgor, with its 12thC church and 19thC inn, an attractive section of the Offa's Dyke Path, watermills and old bridleways. Allow about 3 hours.

START High Street, Trelawnyd [SJ 091798] or alternatively, Gwaenysgor [SJ 075811].

DIRECTIONS Trelawnyd lies on the A5151 road 2 miles east of Dyserth. In the village centre, by the war memorial and village hall, take the road signposted to Llanasa (High Street), where there is a car park on the right. See **Walk 1** for the alternative start.

Trelawnyd is also known as 'Newmarket' – a name given it by the local entrepreneur John Wynne in 1700 after he enlarged the village and established a weekly market and four annual fairs. He promoted the trades of tanning, nail making, silk weaving and tobacco preparation, but none survived for long. The village economy still largely relied on farming and local lead-mining. The population peaked at 713 in 1841.

1 Walk up High Street, soon swinging RIGHT out of the village to take a path on the left signposted to Gop Hill. Head up the field to cross a stone stile in the corner. Immediately turn LEFT over another stile to follow a permissive path ahead alongside the boundary/wood edge. The path soon rises gently through the wood, before rejoining the boundary at a prominent viewpoint. Continue along the wood edge, soon swinging half-RIGHT through the trees to leave the wood and follow a path across the south-facing slope of the summit cairn on Gop Hill. *The purpose of the bronze age or early*

neolithic cairn (14 metres high and 100 metres wide) is uncertain. Legend associates it with Queen Boadicea's final resting place. Thought to be a burial mound, late 19thC excavations revealed no evidence of burials. However, the remains of 14 neolithic people buried in a crouched position have been found in a cave below the summit. The views are superb, ranging from Blackpool Tower to the mountains of Snowdonia.

2 Return down the path and, after a few yards, drop down RIGHT to go through a kissing-gate. Head half-LEFT down across open pasture to a waymark post. Here turn RIGHT along a level faint green track across the mid-slopes of Gop Hill. The path passes above Gop Farm and a derelict 17thC stone dovecot, before swinging RIGHT to cross a stile at the bottom of the wood. Go half-LEFT over another stile, then head down the middle of a large field, passing a telegraph pole to cross a stile ahead, and on over another stile in the next field corner onto a road. Follow it RIGHT into Gwaenysgor.

Gwaenysgor is an ancient settlement, whose 12thC Church of St. Mary Magdalene stands on an important pre-Roman religious site, denoted by its circular churchyard. It holds the only unbroken parish records in Wales, which dates from 1538. At the staggered crossroads, turn LEFT to reach The Eagle and Child. Dating from 1831, the inn takes its name from the legend of a medieval nobleman who persuaded his wife to adopt his illegitimate child, alleging it had been found in an eagle's nest on his estate.

3 Continue along the lane and down a stony track to join a waymarked path through three fields to cross a stile at a prominent viewpoint. Follow an old fence down to cross a hidden stile, then turn LEFT to walk along a path through an area of gorse to join Offa's Dyke Path, which is followed for nearly 2 miles. Keep with the path (Acorn sign) as it contours along the hillside, passing the edge of a quarry and through a small wood, and on to pass by the appropriately named Red Roofs, to reach a lane.

4 Turn LEFT, then LEFT again at the junction to cross a stile up on the right. Now follow the waymarked path through the next four fields to drop down to a lane. Follow it LEFT, then soon cross a stile on your right. Head up the field and on across the next to reach the A5151. Cross the road and a stile almost opposite to go through a field to a lane. Follow it RIGHT and just beyond some cottages – *note the ruin of Grove Mill below* – continue ahead along a track signposted to Cwm, passing a trout farm to reach Marian Mill. *The fast flowing stream – a good source*

of watercress – once turned the waterwheels of these mills for generating power for turning corn into flour and for the fulling process in the preparation of yarns and woven fabric.

5 Swing RIGHT alongside old railings (or to shorten the walk follow a bridleway left along the valley) and by a small stone building, leave Offa's Dyke Path by continuing alongside the railings to follow an enclosed bridleway to a road. Follow it LEFT and, just beyond Plasse Farm, cross a stile on the left. Head half-RIGHT across the large field. *The sheer scale of the summit cairn on Gop Hill can now be fully appreciated.* Cross a stile in the far boundary, then turn LEFT to follow an enclosed bridleway. After it is joined by the alternative bridleway by a stream, it becomes narrower and more attractive

in character. At a waymarked junction, turn LEFT, then soon turn RIGHT over a stile and go through two fields to a lane. Follow it LEFT. *Ahead is the church of St. Michael and All Angels, dating from 1724. On its south side is a 13thC preaching cross.* Now turn RIGHT along the A5151 back to the start.

5

WALK 3
MAES-MYNAN & PWLL-GWYN WOODS

DESCRIPTION A figure of eight 5½ mile walk which explores the attractive and varied countryside overlooking the Wheeler valley, offering good views. The route rises from Afonwen – with an option to visit a nature reserve – to the ancient township of Caerwys, before meandering around the valley edges, and visiting attractive woodland. Allow about 3 hours. The route can easily be shortened to a 3½ mile walk from Afonwen or undertaken as two separate circuits from Caerwys.

START Afonwen Craft/Antique Centre [SJ 131713] or alternatively Caerwys Square [SJ 129731].

DIRECTIONS Afonwen straddles the A541 Mold-Denbigh road. The Centre lies on the south side and is well signposted. Parking is allowed *09.30 - 17.30 Tuesday - Friday with permission, but not at weekends or Bank Holidays.* For the alternative start, take the B5122 from Afonwen up to Caerwys and park in the square.

A fonwen developed as an industrial village during the 18thC with the establishment of a wire works, and a papermill, employing up to 150 people and producing high quality paper for bank notes, legal documents, and Parliamentary notepaper. In the 1930s the mill served as a leatherworks producing gloves, and in the 1960s became a textile and woollen mill. The mill is now a popular Craft and Antique Centre, with a restaurant and Holistic Treatment facilities, and is well worth a visit.

1 Return to the A541, turn LEFT and take the road opposite signposted to Babell, passing houses to cross a stile straight ahead on the bend. Follow the edge of a wood to cross a stile by a gate and on through the

next field to cross another stile. The path now continues ahead through or by areas of hawthorn and on past the entrance to an old sandstone quarry, and then along a track to a road. (*Here, you can follow the lane opposite to visit Y Ddol Uchaf Nature Reserve*). Turn LEFT along the road. Just after Bryn Sinion cottage take a path on the right by an old lime kiln. It rises steadily through the trees and on to rejoin the road. Turn RIGHT, soon passing a wooden 'totem pole'.

2 After passing a ruin, cross a stile on the left. Go across the field and over a stile in the boundary ahead. Follow the field edge on the left to cross a stile in the boundary. Head half-RIGHT across the middle of the next field towards Caerwys church tower, to drop down through gorse and over a stile. Now follow the edge of a wood down to cross a stile in the field corner. Follow the path through the trees to turn LEFT over a stile by Seven Springs Fishery – *formerly the site of a leather works. (The owner will appreciate people not lingering, as this aggravates his dogs).* Go up the access lane and along the road to Caerwys square. *Turning right will bring you to the 17thC Piccadilly Inn, given by Lord Mostyn in gratitude to the jockey of his horse, named Piccadilly, after it won a local race.*

C aerwys, lying on a limestone plateau, was a leading Welsh market town, trading and legal centre from 1290, when Edward I granted a Royal Charter, until the 17thC. It played an important role in Welsh cultural life in the 16thC by hosting eisteddfodau in 1523 and 1568. It was also on the old Pilgrim's route between Holywell and St. David's in Pembrokeshire. Whilst largely untouched by the industrial revolution, it retained its importance as a animal market well into the 20thC.

3 Go along High Street opposite, passing 16thC Bell House – *which takes its name from the bell once mounted in a window overlooking the square and rung on the arrival of funeral processions, and on fair and market days, when holly hung outside the door indicated it was open for the sale of*

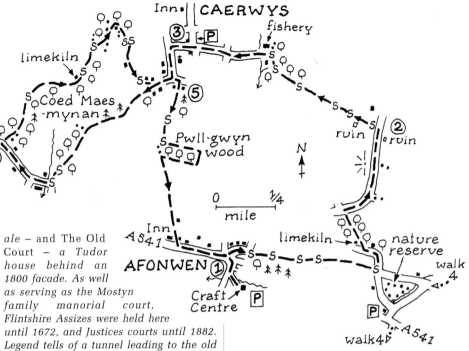

ale – and The Old Court – *a Tudor house behind an 1800 facade. As well as serving as the Mostyn family manorial court, Flintshire Assizes were held here until 1672, and Justices courts until 1882. Legend tells of a tunnel leading to the old gaol.* At a junction turn LEFT, beyond 14thC St Michael's church. At the bend, turn RIGHT along a track. (*For the shorter route, turn left and resume text at point* **5**). Keep ahead at a path junction, following a delightful enclosed path along the edge of a golf course. The path skirts the edge of Coed Maes-mynan as it steadily descends to cross a stile at the bottom of the wood by a stream. Continue along a field edge to the bend of a road. Follow the road RIGHT, passing Maes-mynan farm, soon rising steadily by a quarry entrance and old quarry buildings.

4 Take a waymarked path on the right through trees to follow a clear path rising along the western edge of Coed Maes-mynan. After crossing a stile follow the wood boundary on your right to cross another stile above a small quarry and old lime kiln. Continue along the wood edge and, just before a field corner, cross a stile on your right. Drop down through the trees to join a wider path. Follow it LEFT and, after about 40 yards, follow a lower path on the right down to the bottom of the deep wooded valley. Then swing RIGHT to follow a fence round a small sewage works. Just beyond the end of the fence, take a path rising LEFT to leave the wood by a stile. Go across a narrow golf link, through a gateway, then turn RIGHT to follow the edge of the golf course around to cross a stile in the field corner. Follow a track LEFT to the road. Continue ahead along the road for a few yards.

5 Turn RIGHT on a path between houses and follow a half-walled track to cross a stile at its end. Continue ahead along a field edge to reach Pwll-gwyn Nature Reserve – *an attractive area of woodland, owned by The Woodland Trust.* Turn LEFT by a noticeboard to follow a circular path around its edge to rejoin the main path, which you follow LEFT down to the A541 by the Pwll-gwyn Hotel – *a 16thC coaching inn.* Turn LEFT along the road to reach the Centre. *Note the large Victorian milestone and trough on the right.*

WALK 4
BRYN GOLAU & YSCEIFIOG LAKE

DESCRIPTION A delightful 6½ mile walk exploring the valleys and foothills of the Clwydians, with good views, using little known paths, bridleways and quiet lanes. The route takes in both sides of the Wheeler valley and visits the ancient village of Ysceifiog, with its traditional country inn and nearby lake, finishing at a nature reserve – a rich habitat for animals, rare plants and insects. Allow about 3½ hours. The route can easily be shortened or undertaken as two separate walks.

START Lay-by on A541 near Afonwen [SJ 143711] or Ysceifiog [SJ 152716].
DIRECTIONS Park in either of two lay-bys situated ¾ mile east of Afonwen on the A541 Mold-Denbigh road. For the alternative start, turn off the A541 to Ysceifiog, where roadside parking is available.

1 Take the minor road located between the lay-bys heading south towards the hills. Soon turn LEFT to follow an attractive rising lane – *offering good views over the Wheeler valley*. Shortly after passing Tyn y Pwll, turn sharp RIGHT along a track. *Prominent on the skyline to the north is Ysceifiog church.* Follow the track past a cottage, then when it splits take the LEFT fork to pass just above a house. Follow this delightful green track as it rises steadily up the open hillside alongside a fence – *soon offering extensive open views. To the west is Moel y Parc with its TV. transmitter mast, and further south, Penycloddiau*.

2 At the top of the rise, when you can see a farm directly ahead, go half-LEFT across the open hillside, then drop down to the boundary in line with the farm, and on with the fence to go through a gate in the field corner. Continue ahead, following the boundary on your right round to pass above the farm and on through a gate by a small plantation. Continue down the farm's access track to swing LEFT along a lane. After passing Hen Living, just beyond a wood, bear half-LEFT along a track to pass through a gate. Continue with the enclosed bridleway as it heads along the Disgynfa valley. After passing a track to a cottage you will reach a major fork in the track.

3 Here you cross a gate on your left and head half-LEFT up and across the field to pass through a gate in the corner (*this can be muddy*). Follow the boundary on the left to cross a stile in the top field corner, and on through the next field to cross another stile at the top of the rise – *with extensive views of Moel y Parc, Penycloddiau, Moel Arthur, and Moel Plas-yw, and of Beeston and Peckforton hills in Cheshire to the east.* Continue ahead across the next two open fields, and on along a delightful tree-lined path, before dropping down through trees to pass a former Methodist chapel. Continue down a track to join a lane. (*To shorten the walk turn left, soon returning along your outward route*). Follow it down to cross over the former Mold – Denbigh railway line and river Wheeler at Sarn.

4 Cross the A541 and head up the lane opposite, then turn RIGHT to follow a rising bridleway which passes houses to reach a lane. Follow it LEFT, soon turning RIGHT over a stile. Follow the field edge ahead and on through a wood, then head half-LEFT to follow a path through several fields to enter the corner of 19thC St Mary's churchyard by a 'gravestone' stile. *Behind a tree on the right is the remains of an old preaching cross.* Leave the churchyard by the main gate and head down towards the Fox Inn – *a traditional 18thC country inn with an open fire and serving real ale.*

Ysceifiog, *a remote, tiny, and ancient settlement set 600ft above sea-level, and mentioned in the Doomsday Book, has an interesting history. It developed mainly as an agricultural community, but has prospered from its diversity of natural resources.*

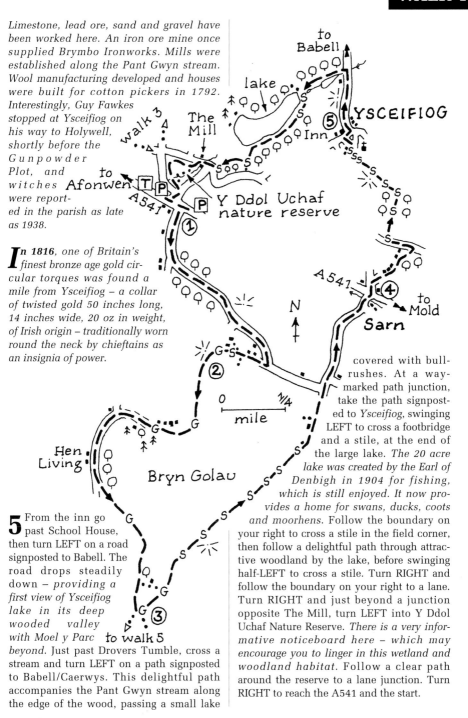

Limestone, lead ore, sand and gravel have been worked here. An iron ore mine once supplied Brymbo Ironworks. Mills were established along the Pant Gwyn stream. Wool manufacturing developed and houses were built for cotton pickers in 1792. Interestingly, Guy Fawkes stopped at Ysceifiog on his way to Holywell, shortly before the Gunpowder Plot, and witches were reported in the parish as late as 1938.

*I*n 1816, one of Britain's finest bronze age gold circular torques was found a mile from Ysceifiog – a collar of twisted gold 50 inches long, 14 inches wide, 20 oz in weight, of Irish origin – traditionally worn round the neck by chieftains as an insignia of power.

to Babell

lake

The Mill

to Afonwen

walk 3

Y Ddol Uchaf nature reserve

YSCEIFIOG

Inn

A541

N

A541

to Mold

Sarn

mile

Hen Living

Bryn Golau

5 From the inn go past School House, then turn LEFT on a road signposted to Babell. The road drops steadily down – *providing a first view of Ysceifiog lake in its deep wooded valley with Moel y Parc* to walk 5 beyond. Just past Drovers Tumble, cross a stream and turn LEFT on a path signposted to Babell/Caerwys. This delightful path accompanies the Pant Gwyn stream along the edge of the wood, passing a small lake

to walk 5

covered with bullrushes. At a waymarked path junction, take the path signposted to Ysceifiog, swinging LEFT to cross a footbridge and a stile, at the end of the large lake. *The 20 acre lake was created by the Earl of Denbigh in 1904 for fishing, which is still enjoyed. It now provides a home for swans, ducks, coots and moorhens.* Follow the boundary on your right to cross a stile in the field corner, then follow a delightful path through attractive woodland by the lake, before swinging half-LEFT to cross a stile. Turn RIGHT and follow the boundary on your right to a lane. Turn RIGHT and just beyond a junction opposite The Mill, turn LEFT into Y Ddol Uchaf Nature Reserve. *There is a very informative noticeboard here – which may encourage you to linger in this wetland and woodland habitat.* Follow a clear path around the reserve to a lane junction. Turn RIGHT to reach the A541 and the start.

WALK 5
MOEL ARTHUR & PENYCLODDIAU

DESCRIPTION An exhilarating 8 mile walk to two stunning iron-age hillforts on a route that explores the beautiful, yet little known, eastern valleys and foothills of the Clwydians, with extensive and ever changing views throughout. Allow about 4 hours. The route can easily be undertaken as two shorter circuits of 4½ or 5 miles.

START Llangwyfan Forestry car park [SJ 139668].

DIRECTIONS From Mold, take the A541 towards Denbigh, then turn off left for Nannerch. Take the first road left, signposted Llandyrnog, for about 3 miles. The car park is on the right at the top of the pass by the forest.

1 From the car park, continue along the road, then turn LEFT on Offa's Dyke Path (Acorn sign). Cross a stile and head straight up the steep grassy slope to cross two further stiles. The path now rises less steeply to reach the shoulder of Moel Arthur. Just before the path begins to descend, turn RIGHT to follow a path to the top of the hill through the original fort entrance.

The conical heather-covered hill of Moel Arthur (1494 ft) is crowned by a small, but prominent iron-age hillfort, defended on the naturally weaker northern side by two impressive ramparts and ditches. There is evidence of hut circles, and a hoard of Bronze Age copper axes have been found here. The views on a clear day of coast, mountains and hills stretching from the Pennines to Snowdonia are superb.

Retrace your steps to follow Offa's Dyke Path down to a road in the next valley.

2 Follow the road LEFT, soon turning RIGHT to follow a track alongside the for-

est edge. At the end of the forest continue on the track. At the top of a slight rise, at a bend, turn LEFT through the middle of three gates to follow an enclosed bridleway on a gradual descent. Just beyond the remains of an old barn, turn LEFT over a stile and follow the field edge to cross another stile by a wood corner. Now, head half-RIGHT down the field to reach a fence just above a stream. Follow the fence LEFT to cross it via a stile. Head half-LEFT, cross the stream, and keep half-LEFT a little way up the field, before swinging LEFT to cross a stile. Go half-RIGHT to reach a road. *Ahead up the wooded valley are unfamiliar views of Moel Llys-y-*

coed, Moel Arthur and Moel Plas-yw. Turn LEFT, then cross a stile on your right.

3 Continue ahead by the remains of an old boundary, soon dropping down to cross a stile. Head half-LEFT to cross a stream by a field corner. Follow the boundary up the field to pass through a gate by a forest corner. Follow a track along the forest edge, soon dropping down and swinging RIGHT past outbuildings and a cottage, and on to meet another track. Turn LEFT, and follow the delightful tree-lined track rising steadily up the valley side. After passing through a gate just beyond a ruined cottage, head half-RIGHT up open ground, *soon reaching a superb viewpoint of Penycloddiau and the northern Clwydians.* Continue in the same direction, dropping steadily down the open hillside to go through a gate in the field corner, and on with the fence to cross a stile. Now head half-LEFT down to cross a stile by a gate, and follow a track down the field edge. At the fence corner above Bryn-ffynnon farm, leave the track to drop down to cross a stile on the right. Head down half-LEFT to go through a small wooden gate on the right side of an outbuilding, and on over a stile to follow the access lane RIGHT to road.

4 Go through the gate opposite, and follow the boundary on the left. At its end, turn LEFT over a stream and on to cross a stile and another stream. Go up the field edge, over a stile and on up to pass through a gate into the field above. Follow the boundary on the right up the field to cross a stile ahead, and on by a house and over a stile in the field corner. Cross the stile ahead and **4** drop down to cross a stile by an old chalet. Drop down steeply to cross a footbridge and stile. Follow the field edge and go up the slope ahead. Cross a stile and continue uphill to follow a fence on the left to go through a gap in the field corner.

5 Now follow the fence half-LEFT round to cross a stile by a stream. Go half-LEFT to walk alongside an old wall, passing a ruin, and through a gate. Now, continue with the wall on your right, on a path skirting beneath Penycloddiau. After passing through another gate, follow a delightful rising green path round to meet a track. Turn LEFT, passing a farm entrance, and when the track swings right, cross a stile on the left by a gate to rejoin Offa's Dyke Path. Head half-LEFT up the slope, passing a clump of trees, and simply follow the superb well waymarked ridge path rising steadily to the summit of Penycloddiau, with its iron-age fort, and extensive views, before continuing on a gradual descent back to the start.

***P**enycloddiau means 'The hill of the trenches'. Its hill-fort is the largest on the Clwydians and one of the largest in Wales. The interior is ½ mile long and encloses an area of some 24 hectares, within a single substantial grass-covered rampart, strengthened at its northern end. There is evidence of level hut platforms within the fort.*

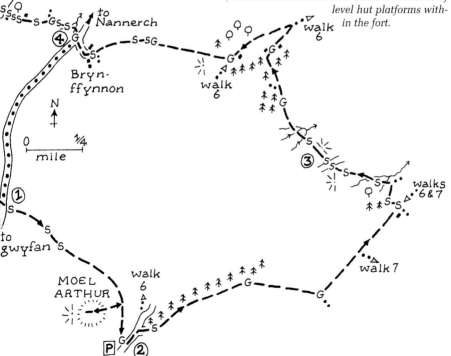

WALK 6
MOEL PLAS-YW

DESCRIPTION This 5 mile walk, with excellent views, rises steadily from the Wheeler valley on an attractive old enclosed bridleway to follow an open green track to the pass beneath Moel Arthur and Moel Llys-y-Coed. It then returns across the open slopes of Moel Plas-yw and through the attractive Penbedw estate. Allow about 2¾ hours. The walk includes an optional extension to the top of Moel Arthur.

START Lay-by on A541 Mold – Denbigh road. [SJ 680173] or alternatively the car park beneath Moel Arthur [SJ 148658].

DIRECTIONS From Mold take the A541 towards Denbigh. After about 6 miles, shortly after passing the turn-off for Cilcain and another minor road by a lodge, park in a lay-by on the left. For the alternative start, follow the minor road to the top of the pass beneath Moel Arthur.

1 From the lay-by walk east along the road towards Mold, using available pavements. *In the field adjoining the lay-by, near some trees are the remains of a stone circle. Its origin is still uncertain.* Take the second road on the right signposted to Cilcain. At the first bend, go up a track passing the entrance to Tardd-y-dwr to follow a bridleway. Just past Siamber Wen, when the bridleway splits, swing RIGHT (it can be muddy here). The bridleway soon begins to rise steadily, becoming more stony in character, passing an old barn, to eventually end at a gate. Go through the gate onto a broad green track. Turn RIGHT and follow the track across open country – *with good views* – then alongside the edge of a forest, to reach a minor road at the high pass lying between Moel Llys-y-Coed and Moel Arthur.

*F**or** those with time and energy to spare, who wish to extend the walk to take in nearby Moel Arthur with its iron-age fort, follow the road left to the car park, then take a waymarked path rising over the shoulder of Moel Arthur. At a marker post near a wooden gate, follow a path left through the origi-*nal entrance of the fort to the summit. See **Walk 5** *for further information. Retrace your steps to resume the main walk.*

2 Turn RIGHT along the road and, after about 100 yards, go through a gate on the left by a waymark post, to follow a green track rising up the hillside – *soon enjoying good views down the part wooded valley, north-east towards Merseyside, and east to Beeston and Peckforton hills in Cheshire, and on a clear day the Pennines beyond.* At the top of the rise the track levels out and then drops down to skirt the western slopes of Moel Plas-yw, alongside a fence on the left, to end at a gate. *This section offers extensive new views: west over the Vale of Clwyd and Denbigh Moors to the mountains of Snowdonia; north-west to nearby Penycloddiau, with its iron-age fort, and Moel y Parc with its T.V. transmitter mast; and north to the coast.*

3 Go through the gate, and walk straight ahead across an area of open pasture alongside an old field boundary on your left. Pass a small wood, go through a gate, and continue with a track dropping gently down to pass through another gate by a wood and a ruined cottage. Continue with the track – *offering good views* – as it descends through a delightful avenue of majestic mature trees. *Lower down the track, there are fine views across open undulating countryside towards Mold, and Moel Famau, with its ruined Jubilee Tower – the highest point on the Clwydian Range, but looking less imposing from this viewpoint.* Follow the track down, crossing a cattle-grid and passing a small wood and old barn. *Ahead lie the various buildings of Penbedw. The original grand 18thC Penbedw Hall became derelict and was demolished in 1958.* Continue ahead to pass to the right of the front of an elegant brick house, to go through a gateway onto a driveway. Follow the drive to the RIGHT, soon passing the remains of a large walled garden. *In the field to your right is a tumulus – an ancient burial site which revealed a burial urn when opened in 1860.* When you reach the A541, turn RIGHT and walk WITH CARE along the road edge the few hundred yards back to the start.

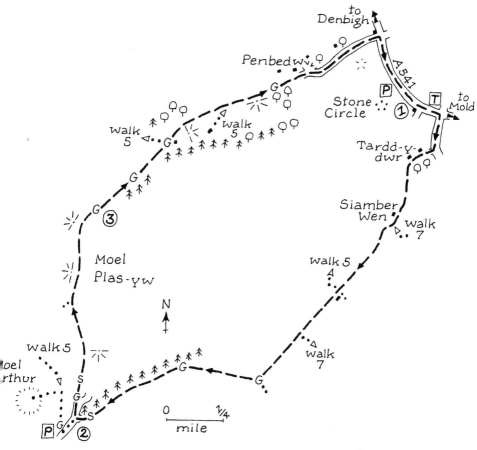

If you have enjoyed the walks in this book, why not try others in the series!

WALK 7
ALYN VALLEY & COED DDU

DESCRIPTION A meandering 7 mile walk, exploring the attractive and varied countryside between Hendre and Cilcain, utilising several delightful old bridleways. The route starts from a traditional 17thC inn, rising from the Wheeler valley through open countryside to the ancient hillside settlement of Cilcain with its medieval church and 16thC inn. It then visits the narrow wooded Alyn valley – a Site of Special Scientific Interest – before returning through the attractive woodland of Coed Ddu and passing a woodland reserve. Allow about 3½ hours. The Alyn valley and adjoining limestone area became a major part of north-east Wales' lead-mining industry from the 17th to the 19th centuries.
START The Royal Oak, Hendre [SJ 189677].
DIRECTIONS The Royal Oak lies on the A541 about 5 miles west of Mold. Parking is allowed in the car park, but the landlord will appreciate being informed in advance. (tel. 01352 741466). *Please park tidily.*

1 From the Royal Oak – *once used as a Coroners Court following the death of miners at Cilcain* – go to the nearby side road, then walk between Tollbar and Oak cottages to follow a path through the trees, passing old quarry structures. Continue on a bridleway along the edge of a wood, passing a lime kiln, to swing LEFT by Ty-isaf – *an old hall house* – along its access track to a road. Go up the track opposite, by Hilltop to follow an enclosed bridleway. When it meets another bridleway, follow it LEFT (*the initial section can be muddy in wet conditions*). It soon begins to rise steadily, becoming more stony in character, to pass an old barn (*where there is an alternative path to point 2*). Eventually turn LEFT along a waymarked bridleway, soon passing through trees, over a stream, and on to join a lane. Follow the lane to a road junction and turn RIGHT.

2 Follow the road, keeping ahead at the next junction to cross a stile ahead on the bend by a pumping station. Now go ahead to follow a waymarked path through several fields to reach the village hall and road at Cilcain. *St Mary's church opposite, dating from the 14thC, contains many interesting features, including a magnificent carved oak roof with winged angels, and is well worth a visit.* Turn LEFT to the White Horse – *a 16thC coaching inn* – where refreshments are available. *A piece of gold found in the nearby hills in 1889 created a short-lived 'gold rush' with several tiny mines opening. Sadly, one owned by the inn landlord failed to make him rich, being worked out after only six months!*

3 At the crossroads, follow the road ahead towards Pantymwyn. After ½ mile, turn LEFT on a side road by Wallacre, then cross a stile on your right. Follow the boundary on your left to drop down the second field to go through a gate in the corner. Head half-RIGHT to drop down to cross a stile onto a junction of bridleways. Go up the enclosed bridleway opposite, through a gate, then swing RIGHT to pass in front of a cottage and on along its access track to a lane. Immediately go down a track to follow an enclosed path passing beneath the gate to Pandy down through the trees. When the path swings right down towards the river Alyn, turn LEFT up the bank past a metal post to follow a path through the wood, soon dropping down to cross a large footbridge over the river. *Ahead is the imposing limestone cliff of Pandy quarry which closed in 1950. It was originally the site of the great ironmaster John Wilkinson's Llyn y Pandy lead-mine, which he took over in 1791. The mine, which attracted Cornish workers, produced good yields of lead, which was probably shipped to his lead piping factory in London. However flooding remained a constant problem despite the efforts of four large steam engines, and contributed to its demise.* Turn LEFT, soon joining a clear track that rises above houses, then continue up a waymarked track through the trees. At a waymark post, turn LEFT to follow the lower of two paths, descending steadily through the trees to join a track above the river. Follow it RIGHT to cross the river to a road.

ahead over two further stiles to follow an access track to a road. Follow the road ahead for ⅓ mile.

4 Follow it ahead and, after 30 yards, take a path angling sharp LEFT up the valley side. Cross a stile and follow the path up to go through a small gate. Continue ahead, passing a house to follow white waymark posts to cross a stile by a gate. Cross the access track and a stile opposite. Follow the field edge to enter Coed Ddu by a stile. *The nearby house of the same name is where, in 1829, the composer Mendelssohn stayed as guest of John Taylor, the mining engineer.* Turn LEFT and follow a delightful path through the wood to a waymarked path junction at the wood edge. Follow the RIGHT-hand path through the wood to a multi-way-marked path junction. Take the path straight ahead to swing RIGHT on a stony track to follow a well waymarked trail by a ruined house to leave the wood by a stile. Continue

5 Just beyond Vardo, as the road begins to descend, turn LEFT along a track (soon passing a short cut to Hendre) to reach Big Wood, which is owned by the Woodland Trust. *A circular path allows you to explore the wood, which contains a variety of trees and the remains of late 19thC lead mining activity.* Continue along the track to its end at the entrance to Mwynbwll farm. Go through the gateway and cross a stile directly ahead, then go half-RIGHT to pass to the right of a ruin. Continue down through trees to go through a gate ahead. Carry on ahead for about 100 yards to join a delightful enclosed bridleway, which you follow by a house to drop gently down to a waymark post. Here you swing sharp RIGHT to return along your outward route, for a welcome drink at the Royal Oak.

WALK 8
MOEL FAMAU

DESCRIPTION A 5 mile walk from just outside Cilcain to Moel Famau, the highest point on the Clwydian Range (1820 ft) which offers extensive views. This is one of the most enjoyable and less demanding routes to the summit, using delightful scenic bridleways and good paths. Allow about 3 hours.
START Waterworks ⅓ mile south-west of Cilcain. [SJ 172648]
DIRECTIONS From the A541 Mold – Denbigh road take the road to Cilcain. In the village centre, turn right past the White Horse Inn, then left by the church. Follow this minor road down to park near waterworks.

1 From the bend of the road go up the driveway to Tyddyn-y-foel then, after a few yards, cross a stile on the right. Follow the boundary on the left through two fields to reach a track junction. Turn LEFT to follow a bridleway along a track, soon crossing a stream by a gate, and on up the hillside to pass through another gate. Continue directly ahead, soon over a wooden raised walkway across a marshy area. This delightful bridleway then contours round the hillside – *providing open views across to Cilcain, Halkyn Mountain and east towards Cheshire* – to pass a cottage.

2 Beyond the cottage, and just before a gate ahead, swing sharp RIGHT up another waymarked bridleway. Follow this bridleway, enclosed by a fence/wall on the left and the remains of an old boundary on the right, as it rises steadily up the open slopes of Ffrith Mountain. *After a while the summit of Moel Famau with its distinctive ruined Jubilee Tower comes into view on the skyline ahead.* The bridleway rises to follow the edge of a forestry plantation, soon levelling out to pass through a gate. Continue ahead and, at the end of the plantation, by a waymark post, turn LEFT to rise steadily alongside the forest edge, before beginning a final short steeper ascent to reach the north-east

corner of the tower at the top of Moel Famau

Moel Famau, meaning 'Mother's Mountain', is the highest point in the Clwydian range. The remains of the Jubilee Tower are a recognised landmark seen from Snowdonia, Cheshire and Merseyside. It was built in 1810, by public subscription, to commemorate George III's 50 years as king. The original 115 foot tower, designed by Thomas Harrison of Chester and the first Egyptian-style monument to be built in Britain, must have been one of the most striking sights in North Wales. Only the base remains, the obelisk having been blown down by storms on 27th October 1862. The 360-degree views are breathtaking. On a clear day, they range from Snowdon to the Cheshire Plain and Shropshire hills; from Cader Idris to Blackpool Tower and the Lakeland Fells. Metal information boards set in the viewing platform of the Jubilee Tower will locate the extensive sights to be seen.

3 From the north-west corner of the tower, drop down a few yards west towards the Vale of Clwyd, then swing half-RIGHT down to a waymark post at the end of a section of wooden fencing. Now follow the main ridge along Offa's Dyke path, signposted to Moel Dywyll. Follow the clear path, soon descending the heather-covered slope, to continue on the level alongside a boundary wall on the right. After a few hundred yards, the path drops down to a small hollow by a waymark post. Here, turn RIGHT through a small wooden gate to follow a path passing a small pond as it contours around the heather-covered hillside alongside the remains of an old wall on the left. *In the valley below is one of several reservoirs to be found in the area.* The path passes through a gap in a cross wall. Ignore a path leading off left with this wall, but continue ahead with what is now a bridleway, soon running between two old boundary walls for a short section, before the right-hand wall peters out.

4 When you reach the waymark post met earlier, by the end of the forest, turn sharp LEFT on a clear path descending down towards a side valley containing a small reservoir. The path drops down steeply at first, before levelling out to pass through a gate just before the reservoir. Follow the path on a gradual descent to cross a stile by a gate, and continue along an enclosed bridleway. When it meets another track, by your outward route, follow it LEFT down past a house to a track junction. Turn RIGHT on a bridleway along the track back to the start.

walk 7

CILCAIN Inn ▸ walk 7

walk 9

waterworks

① Tyddyn-y -foel

reservoir

② walk 9

N

0   ¼
mile

④

G

The Jubilee Tower – as it probably looked when complete

③ Jubilee Tower

Moel Famau

CILCAIN

walk 7 Inn

walk

④

Loggerheads has been popular with visitors since the early 19th C. The Crosville Motor Bus Company acquired land in 1926

and established tea-rooms, gardens, bandstand and boating lake for day-trippers. In 1974, it was established as a Country Park covering 74 acres of the Alyn valley, and today offers a visitor centre, restaurant, outdoor shop, and restored watermill.

River Alyn

⑤

walk 8

Ffrith

walk 8

Ffrith Mountain

③

short cut

kennels

to Moel Famau

Brithdir Mawr

N

②

0   ¼
mile

1 Walk back along the drive then, at a house, take a path half-RIGHT to a road. Follow the road RIGHT. *Ahead lie the tree-covered slopes of Moel Famau.* At a T-junction, turn RIGHT, then in a dip, turn LEFT through a 'private' gate by a stream, and follow a track along the attractive side valley. After about ½ mile, turn LEFT up a rough track leading to a house, then cross a stile on the right, signposted to Moel Famau. Head slightly LEFT to cross a stile by a forest. Turn RIGHT along the forest edge, soon crossing a ladder stile, then at a waymark post, head down to cross the stream.

2 Follow the fence on your right, and when it bends right, continue straight ahead by a waymark post. Now swing half-LEFT across open ground to follow a path parallel with a stream. In the field corner, cross the stream and a stile, then continue on a bridle-way to reach a waymarked path rising through the trees to Moel Famau (*offering an optional direct there and back ascent or link to **Walk 8***). Continue ahead with the bridle-

18

WALK 9
FFRITH MOUNTAIN & THE ALYN GORGE

way, soon swinging RIGHT over a stream, and on along a steadily improving track to pass Brithdir-mawr – a 16thC hall house. Continue along its access lane, then take a bridleway LEFT past Bryn Ffynnon. (*For the shorter walk continue down the lane to a road, then follow a path opposite down to cross the river, and rise half-right to rejoin the main walk on the leete path*).

3 Follow the bridleway past Ffrith farm, (and then an alternative waymarked field path to Cilcain), before swinging west around the northern slopes of Ffrith Mountain. After going through a gate marked 'Castell', the bridleway splits. Take the RIGHT fork. The bridleway passes a cottage, then contours round the hillside – *offering fine open views of Cilcain* – before dropping steadily down to cross a stream. At a way-marked bridleway/path junction, cross a stile on the right. Walk through the edge of two fields to a farm's access track. Turn LEFT, then continue up the road into Cilcain.

Cilcain is an ancient hillside settlement sited at a meeting point of old drover's roads. St. Mary's 14thC church contains many interesting features, including a magnificent carved oak roof with winged angels. The White Horse, a 16thC coaching inn, makes a good refreshment stop.

4 Turn RIGHT at the crossroads by the inn, and follow the road down to take a way-marked bridleway on the left, passing above trout pools. Near the stream, take a path rising half-LEFT through the trees, then follow a way-marked path above the edge of the deep wooded valley to reach a road. Follow it down, over the river, and half-way up the hill, take a path on the right signposted to Loggerheads.

5 Now simply follow the 'Leete Path' for two miles along the beautiful Alyn gorge – *a Site of Special Scientific Interest containing major cave systems* – back to Loggerheads. *The path takes its name from*

DESCRIPTION An excellent 7 mile walk exploring beautiful valleys and foothills. The route takes you around Ffrith mountain, with good open views, passes a medieval house, and visits the ancient hillside village of Cilcain, with its medieval church and 16thC coaching inn. It returns down the impressive wooded Alyn valley on the famous 'leete path', passing limestone crags and old lead mines – scenery enjoyed by the writer Charles Kingsley and said to inspire Mendelssohn to write *The Rivulet*. Allow about 4 hours. The route can easily be short-ened to 4 mile walk, or extended by 1¾ miles to include a climb up Moel Famau.
START Loggerheads Country Park Centre [SJ 198626] or Cilcain [SJ 172648].
DIRECTIONS Loggerheads lies on the A494 Mold-Ruthin road, 2 miles from Mold. The Park is well signposted and has a large car park. See **Walk 8** for the alternative start.

the distinctive 'leat' – a water channel, origi-nally 2 metres wide and 1.5 deep, built in 1823 by Cornish mining engineer John Taylor, whose Mold Mines Company acquired lead mines in the area. Its purpose was to divert water from the river at Loggerheads past swallow holes in the lime-stone bed, into which the river disappears part of the year, to service waterwheels that powered mining machinery and waterpumps in the mines lower in the valley. It ceased to operate in 1845. Keep with the level leete path high above the Alyn river, passing lime-stone crags, impressive old lead workings, and through attractive mature deciduous woodland, to eventually cross a road. Continue along a track, by kennels, and fol-low the leete path, soon at river level. Cross a stone bridge over the river to return to the Centre.

LOGGERHEADS

19

WALK 10
MOEL FINDEG & DEBORAH'S WELL

DESCRIPTION A 5 mile walk through open country and attractive woodland, with good views throughout. The route visits Maeshafn, before passing through a recently established nature reserve to the summit of Moel Findeg. Although only 1194 ft high, and an easy ascent, it offers commanding panoramic views. Other highlights include an ancient well with a tale to tell, and a choice of country inns on route. Allow about 3 hours.

START Boundary stone monument at Loggerheads [SJ 202626].

DIRECTIONS From Mold take the A494 towards Ruthin. Just past Cadole, as the road descends to Loggerheads, park on the left opposite a large boundary stone monument. Alternatively, continue ¼ mile down the road to Loggerheads Country Park Centre, where there is a large car park. Cross a footbridge over the river by the Centre and walk up the road to the start.

The boundary stone known as 'Carreg Carn March Arthur' (the stone of the hoof of Arthur's horse) has an indentation said to be the hoof print made by King Arthur's magical horse Llamrei on landing after a mighty leap from Moel Famau, fleeing from a Saxon army. The monument above it was erected in 1763 to define the boundary, after a long dispute over mining rights, between the lordships of Mold and Llanferres. This dispute inspired Richard Wilson – a renowned British landscape painter and a founder member of the Royal Academy, who spent his last years at nearby Colomendy Hall – to paint the original sign of the 17thC We Three Loggerheads inn. The sign showed the heads of two gentlemen back to back, as if each is refusing to speak with each other. The missing third 'loggerhead' – equivalent to 'blockhead' today – was meant to be the onlooker! The area takes its name from this famous sign.

1 Opposite the monument, take a path signposted to Maeshafn through the wood to cross a metal stile. *The next section follows a waymarked path through the extensive site of Colomendy Outdoor Education Centre used by children from Merseyside.* Follow a track past outbuildings, and on along a lane, then turn LEFT at a junction. Shortly swing RIGHT along another lane to cross a stile into a field. Continue ahead to enter a wood. Follow a path RIGHT, soon rising gently through the trees. Cross a stile and continue just above the edge of the wood – *soon enjoying open views.* Go through a kissing gate and on past Bryn Tirion to follow a track LEFT to a road. Follow it ahead into Maeshafn – *where refreshments are available at the 17th C Miner's Arms.*

2 Continue through the village, then turn LEFT at a road junction. Shortly, take a road RIGHT to enter Moel Findeg Nature Reserve – *created in 1999 following its purchase by the local authority with the help of villagers, who raised £100,000 to protect it from further quarrying.* Follow a path rising steadily through trees, then more steeply up the open heather and bracken covered hillside to cross a stile onto the summit of Moel Findeg. *The 360-degree views are impressive: north towards the Dee and Mersey estuaries, and the Lancashire hills beyond; east over the Cheshire Plain to Beeston and Peckforton hills; south-west to Shropshire; south to Llandegla Moors; west towards distant Snowdonia.* Continue along the ridge. At its end, drop down half-RIGHT to go past a group of trees and on down the gorse covered slopes towards a farm in the valley below, to pass through a gate by the end of a wood. Continue along the field edge, passing a small pond, to a lane. Turn RIGHT, then LEFT by Haulfryn to follow a delightful track, through a gate, and on past exposed limestone crags, before crossing a stile on the left. Head half-RIGHT across open ground, down past old workings to cross a stile near the field corner. Follow a path down through a wood to a track by houses. Turn RIGHT to reach the A494. *On the right is the Rainbow Inn.*

3 Cross the road to follow the track opposite, passing houses. Beyond a cattle-grid the track rises steadily to follow a field edge – *offering extensive views* – then continues alongside a wood. At a gate, just before a house, cross a stile on the left. Follow the wall round to pass through a gate. Turn LEFT and follow the boundary gently down to cross a stile near a pond and on to a track. Follow it LEFT passing

Map labels: Deborah's Well · walk 9 · walk 9 · Inn · CADOLE · to Mold · **3** · Inn · **4** · **1** Boundary Stone · P · P · LOGGERHEADS · Inn · to Ruthin · Colomendy Centre · N · 0 ¼ mile · Moel Findeg · G · Haulfryn · walk 13 · **2** · MAESHAFN · walk 11 · walk 11 · Inn · walk 13 · walk 12

bungalows, then go RIGHT on a path alongside a cottage, aptly named 'Pathside'. Head across a field to cross a stile in the left corner onto a road. Cross the stile opposite, and follow a path LEFT along the wood edge to *Deborah's Well*. *An engraved plaque records the tale of Deborah, whose efforts in the 16thC to protect local people from cholera ironically led to her death at the hands of those she sought to protect.*

4 Continue along the wood edge to turn RIGHT on a path rising through the trees to a field. Go ahead along the field edge and on up through the tree boundary ahead to swing LEFT to a waymark post. Turn LEFT to follow a woodland path. After crossing a stile, continue ahead, soon on a gentle descent. Keep with the main path, swinging half-LEFT by a small clearing to reach a stile by a chalet – *giving access to the Colomendy Arms*. Turn sharp RIGHT to follow a grey path, past old workings and on to cross a stile. Continue through the trees to meet a cross-path about 100 yards ahead. Follow it down LEFT to a waymark post and on to the road by the start. *Turning RIGHT at the waymark post will take you via a steep stepped path directly back to Loggerheads Centre.*

WALK 11
FRON HEN
& BIG COVERT

DESCRIPTION A varied 5¾ mile walk exploring both sides of the Alyn valley near Llanferres, featuring contrasting open green hills and wooded limestone countryside. The route rises steadily to follow a delightful high-level bridleway round the open slopes of the foothills of Fron Hen, with excellent views, before descending to Llanferres, with its 18thC church and 17thC Inn. It then continues east to the lead-mining village of Maeshafn, with its 17thC inn, before passing through the attractive woodland of Big Covert. Allow about 3 hours. The route can easily be undertaken as two shorter circuits of 3 and 3½ miles.
START Lay-by on A494 Mold-Ruthin road ½ mile south of Llanferres [SJ 187598].
DIRECTIONS Heading towards Ruthin from Llanferres, the large lay-by is on the left, before the Llanarmon-yn-Ial turning.

1 From the Llanferres end of the lay-by, cross the road and go up the track opposite. At the farm entrance, continue ahead over a cattle grid to follow a rising track. When it splits, keep with the RIGHT fork to pass behind a house and chalets to rise steadily up the edge of an attractive side valley. At the top of the rise, when the track swings up towards a farm, continue straight ahead alongside a tree/wall boundary on a waymarked bridleway to go through a gate by the end of a wood. Go along the wood edge and, at its end, swing RIGHT up a bridleway alongside a wall to go through a gate ahead. *The heather-covered hill up to your left is Moel Fenlli, with its iron-age fort.*

2 Continue half-RIGHT to pass through two further gates above a farm, and follow the delightful bridleway round the open slopes of Fron Hen, *offering excellent views: south over the southern Clwydians to Llandegla Moors, Horseshoe Pass, Llantisilio Mountain and the Berwyns beyond; east to Eryrys*

mountain; and later, north-east to Moel Findeg, Deeside, Merseyside, and, on a clear day, the distant Pennines. Shortly after passing through a third gate, the bridleway swings down half-RIGHT. Follow it down – *soon glimpsing Moel Famau ahead* – to eventually pass through a gate by a house on a lane.

3 Immediately turn RIGHT over an adjoining stile, then head across the field to pass a solitary wooden post. Now follow the path by another waymarked post and on through a series of gates behind farm buildings. Follow a track ahead by a small plantation and an area of gorse, and on alongside the fence on your left to drop down to cross a stile at the end of a small forest. Continue ahead down the next field, alongside the fence and stream on your right, to cross the stream and stile in the field corner. Go round the base of the tree in front to follow a path across the field slope past a solitary waymarked post, and on alongside an old boundary to swing LEFT down to go through a gate. *(For a shorter walk cross a nearby stile and follow a path down to the A494).* Now swing LEFT down past the front of a house and follow the access lane down to the A494. *Nearby is the 17thC Druid Inn, where refreshments are available, and the Church of St. Berres, rebuilt in 1774.*

4 Cross the road to a waymark post opposite to go down an enclosed track (*or for a shorter walk follow the road right back to the start*). The track soon runs alongside, then crosses, the river Alyn to go through a gate ahead. Follow the rising enclosed green track, and at its end you have a choice of routes (both indicated). The preferred route is to cross a stile on the left, then turn RIGHT to the field corner, by the attractive black and white Pentre-cerrig-bach before swinging LEFT with the boundary. After about 100 yards strike across the field to cross a ladder-stile ahead. Now follow a path half-RIGHT through an area of shrubs and small trees, over a ladder-stile and on across a small

22

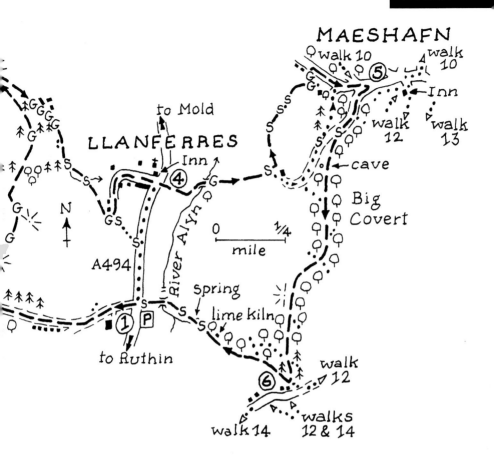

field. Cross another ladder-stile to follow the boundary on your right round to pass through a gate, then go along a track to a lane. Follow the lane RIGHT up to Maeshafn.

5 Just after the 'Maeshafn' sign, turn sharp RIGHT – *or continue to the Miners Arms for refreshments* – to follow a track signposted to Pentre-cerrig through Big Covert wood. After a few hundred yards cross a stile on the left by a gate. *After about 200 yards you will pass a cave hidden down on your right – do not enter. Limited excavation has revealed evidence of human occupation.* Continue with the mainly level path through the wood. At a path junction, take the middle of three tracks, heading half-RIGHT round the wood edge, past an area of cleared forest – *providing a panoramic view. Look for your route round Fron Hen.* At the end of the cleared section, keep straight ahead on the main path, soon dropping down to a path junction. Keep with the main path to swing half-LEFT down to reach a track by a house.

6 Turn RIGHT along the bottom edge of the wood and continue with a green track, passing impressive limestone edges and an old lime kiln to reach a spring. Cross a stile and a stream and follow it to cross a stile in the field corner. Now head half-RIGHT, across a wide flat bridge over the river and up a track to the start.

23

WALK 12
BRYN ALYN

DESCRIPTION A 6 mile figure-of-eight walk exploring the varied countryside between the old lead mining villages of Maeshafn and Eryrys. Highlights includes impressive limestone scenery, open pastureland, attractive woodland, good views, and the opportunity to visit two old country inns. Bryn Alyn, known locally as Pothole Mountain, is a Site of Special Scientific Interest, renowned for its limestone grassland, heath, rock and scree habitats. The hill, rising to 1338 ft, features limestone pavements, ridges, sheer cliff faces, caves, and supports rich flora. Allow about 3 hours. The route can easily be undertaken as two shorter circuits.
START Maeshafn [SJ 202610] or Eryrys [SJ 204578].
DIRECTIONS From Mold take the A494 towards Ruthin then, after about 2 miles take a road left to reach Maeshafn. Park tidily in the village centre. For the alternative start, as you enter Maeshafn, follow the road left past the Youth Hostel to a junction. Follow the road right to Eryrys, then turn right by the Sun Inn, into Caer Odyn, where there is road side parking on the right.

1 Head along the track past the 17thC Miner's Arms and cottages and, at its end, by Pen-y-Ffordd, continue ahead to cross a stile. Follow the fence on your right. Then, at a waymark sign, head half-LEFT up to cross a stile in the field corner, then turn RIGHT over a stile just ahead. Follow the boundary on your left through two fields to cross a stile in the corner. Now go half-RIGHT over an old wall and across the field to cross a stile in the boundary ahead. Continue along a small ridge and across a field to cross a ladder-stile just above a bungalow. Continue ahead alongside the boundary, dropping down to cross a ladder-stile at the wall corner. Follow the path over rough ground to reach a road. Cross a stile opposite and head half-RIGHT up the open green slopes of Bryn Alyn to cross a stile in a fence by an old wall on the shoulder of the hill. Continue ahead

across a small plateau to meet a green track by an old wall/tree boundary.

2 Follow the track LEFT past an area of old lead workings to a road. Turn LEFT, then turn RIGHT along the access track to Fron Deg to cross a stile ahead. Continue ahead on a waymarked path through five fields across Nercwys Mountain, then head half-LEFT to drop down to enter the forest. Follow the path through the forest, and when it meets another path swing RIGHT by the end of a ruin and straight across a track junction. Continue by an area of replanted forest – *offering good views north to the new Dee bridge, Merseyside and the Lancashire coast beyond.* After about 300 yards, turn RIGHT on a faint track for a few yards, then RIGHT again to follow a clear path through the trees. Cross a track, and continue with the rising path to leave the forest by a stile.

3 Head half-LEFT across the field to cross a stile in the corner, and continue half-LEFT to follow the boundary round to cross a stile by a gate, at a good viewpoint. Go ahead to drop down to cross a stile and continue to a tree boundary corner, where you swing LEFT along a track to a lane. Follow it RIGHT, then at a road turn LEFT to cross a stile on your right. Follow the old boundary on your right to go through a field gap, then head half-LEFT round to cross a stile. Turn RIGHT along the field edge for 30 yards, then go half-LEFT to cross a stile in the corner and on over rough ground to a road. Follow it RIGHT into Eryrys. *Note the old village water pump, and the Sun Inn opposite, which now serves as a post office, newsagent, general store and off-licence.*

4 Continue along Caer Odyn to leave the village, passing the Youth Centre. Soon, cross a stile on the right by old sheds. Now follow the boundary on the left up the field, and after about 200 yards, head half-RIGHT across open gorse and limestone covered ground to cross a ladder-stile over a wall on the skyline ahead. *There are extensive views south to Ruabon Mountain, Horseshoe Pass, Llantisilio and Berwyn mountains, and the southern Clwydians.* Continue half-LEFT on

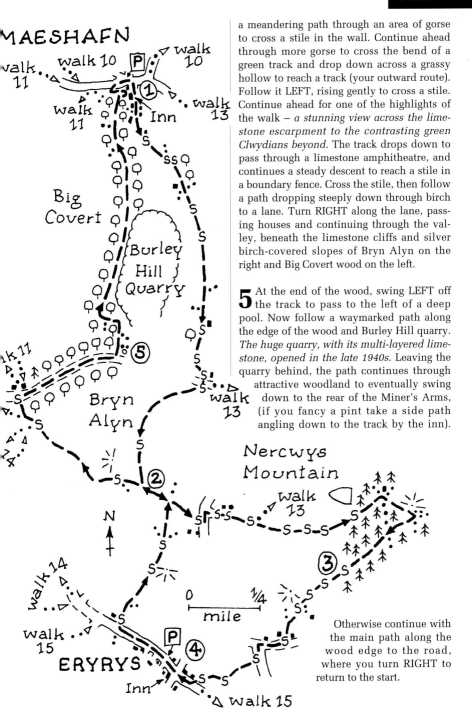

MAESHAFN

walk 11

walk 10

walk 10

walk 11

Inn

walk 13

Big Covert

Burley Hill Quarry

⑤

alk 11

Bryn Alyn

walk 13

N

②

Nercwys Mountain

walk 13

③

walk 14

walk 15

ERYRYS

Inn

④

P

0 ¼ mile

walk 15

a meandering path through an area of gorse to cross a stile in the wall. Continue ahead through more gorse to cross the bend of a green track and drop down across a grassy hollow to reach a track (your outward route). Follow it LEFT, rising gently to cross a stile. Continue ahead for one of the highlights of the walk – *a stunning view across the limestone escarpment to the contrasting green Clwydians beyond.* The track drops down to pass through a limestone amphitheatre, and continues a steady descent to reach a stile in a boundary fence. Cross the stile, then follow a path dropping steeply down through birch to a lane. Turn RIGHT along the lane, passing houses and continuing through the valley, beneath the limestone cliffs and silver birch-covered slopes of Bryn Alyn on the right and Big Covert wood on the left.

5 At the end of the wood, swing LEFT off the track to pass to the left of a deep pool. Now follow a waymarked path along the edge of the wood and Burley Hill quarry. *The huge quarry, with its multi-layered limestone, opened in the late 1940s.* Leaving the quarry behind, the path continues through attractive woodland to eventually swing down to the rear of the Miner's Arms, (if you fancy a pint take a side path angling down to the track by the inn).

Otherwise continue with the main path along the wood edge to the road, where you turn RIGHT to return to the start.

WALK 13
A TALE OF TWO MOUNTAINS

DESCRIPTION A 6¼ mile walk through varied countryside which takes in two 'mountains', with good views throughout. The route crosses Nercwys Mountain – an area of open pasture and woodland, before making an easy ascent to the summit of Moel Findeg (1194 ft) – the 'mountain' saved by villagers, and now a nature reserve. The route returns through attractive limestone country. There is a choice of three country inns on route. Allow about 3½ hours. The route can easily be undertaken as two shorter walks.
START Sun Inn, Eryrys [SJ 204578] or alternatively Maeshafn [SJ 202610].
DIRECTIONS Turn off the A494 Ruthin-Mold road on the B5430 towards Llanarmon-yn-ial. Soon take a road left to Eryrys, then at the Sun Inn, turn left into Caer Odyn, where there is road side parking on the right. For the alternative start see **Walk 12**.

1 From the Sun Inn head towards Mold, pass a side road, then cross a stile on the right just before a white cottage. Head half-LEFT, soon walking alongside a boundary to cross a stile. Go up the field and over the stile ahead, then swing LEFT alongside a tree boundary to cross a stile by a gate. Now go half-RIGHT to cross another stile, and on over gorse-covered pasture towards a distant white house to cross a stile in the field corner. Continue with the fence to cross another stile. Now head half-RIGHT up the next field and round to cross a stile by a small pool onto a lane.

2 Follow the lane LEFT, then turn RIGHT through the gateway of Coed Bach to cross a stile at the end of the garden. Go along an avenue of trees to cross a stile at the edge of the wood, and on by a barn to cross another two stiles, then head half-LEFT down to cross a stile by a gate. Continue ahead to cross a stile on your left. Now head half-RIGHT along a track to cross a stile by a

wooden chalet. Go half-LEFT through the trees, dropping down to cross a stile. Head half-RIGHT, passing through gorse to cross a stile. Go half-RIGHT over rough ground, cross another stile, then follow a clear way-marked path through an area of mixed woodland, soon passing a small pool.

3 Near the edge of the forest, at a way-marked path junction, turn LEFT on a path through the forest to reach a road. *Ahead lies Moel Findeg.* Turn LEFT, then RIGHT along the road towards Maeshafn. After about 200 yards, cross a stile on your right. Follow a green track to swing half-RIGHT to cross a large ladder-stile. Continue half-LEFT rising through gorse to pass behind a house, and on near its access track to cross a stile by a gateway. Continue ahead, over another stile and on to cross a stile by a farm's access track. Now follow the boundary on the left through two fields to a road. Turn RIGHT, passing a Victorian postbox to the Owain Glyndwr Hotel – *where you can sit outside in fine weather to enjoy a drink and superb views.* Retrace your steps and continue along the road.

4 Just beyond Haulfryn, cross a stile on the left, passing a small pond, to go through a gate in the next field corner. Now head half-RIGHT up the open slopes to pass to the left of a small group of trees ahead. Just beyond, go half-RIGHT up onto the rocky top of Moel Findeg. *The panoramic views are impressive, extending from the distant Pennines to Snowdonia.* Continue along the short ridge, over a stile, then follow a path down half-LEFT. When it splits, take the LEFT fork, by a nearby pond, to follow a clear path dropping steadily down through heather, then silver birch to reach a road at the entrance to the reserve. Follow it RIGHT – *to the Miners Arms in Maeshafn if desired.*

5 Otherwise, just past the 'Maeshafn' sign, take a waymarked path LEFT beyond Plas y Ffynnon to cross a stile at the end of its drive. Turn LEFT to follow the boundary through two limestone meadows to cross a stile in the corner. Go RIGHT over another stile just ahead. Follow the boundary on your left through two fields to cross a stile in the corner. Now go half-RIGHT over an old wall and across the field to cross a stile in the boundary ahead. Continue along a small

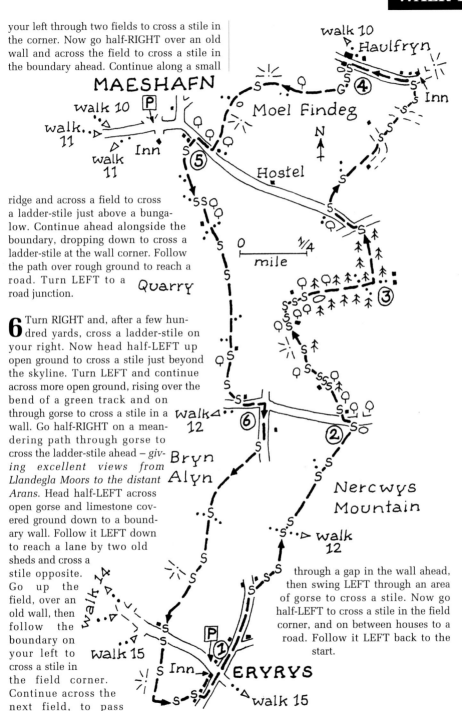

ridge and across a field to cross a ladder-stile just above a bunga-low. Continue ahead alongside the boundary, dropping down to cross a ladder-stile at the wall corner. Follow the path over rough ground to reach a road. Turn LEFT to a road junction.

6 Turn RIGHT and, after a few hun-dred yards, cross a ladder-stile on your right. Now head half-LEFT up open ground to cross a stile just beyond the skyline. Turn LEFT and continue across more open ground, rising over the bend of a green track and on through gorse to cross a stile in a wall. Go half-RIGHT on a mean-dering path through gorse to cross the ladder-stile ahead – *giving excellent views from Llandegla Moors to the distant Arans.* Head half-LEFT across open gorse and limestone cov-ered ground down to a bound-ary wall. Follow it LEFT down to reach a lane by two old sheds and cross a stile opposite. Go up the field, over an old wall, then follow the boundary on your left to cross a stile in the field corner. Continue across the next field, to pass

through a gap in the wall ahead, then swing LEFT through an area of gorse to cross a stile. Now go half-LEFT to cross a stile in the field corner, and on between houses to a road. Follow it LEFT back to the start.

WALK 14
AROUND THE NANT

DESCRIPTION A delightful 5 mile walk exploring the stunning limestone scenery north of Llanarmon-yn-Ial, extensively mined for lead since the 13thC, and possibly in Roman times. This meandering walk takes you past a medieval castle, and two of the area's few surviving mining relics – an impressive engine house and chimney – with options for shortening or varying the route. Allow about 3 hours.

START St Garmon Church, Llanarmon-yn-Ial [SJ 191561].

DIRECTIONS From the A494 Ruthin-Mold road, take the B5430 towards Llanarmon-yn-ial, and after 2 miles turn right on the B5431 to enter the village. Pass the 18thC Raven Inn and the Post Office, to park on the roadside in Maes Ial.

St Garmon's is a medieval double-naved church, extensively restored during the 1730s, with many outstanding features.

1 Follow the B5431 back out of the village, soon dropping down to cross the river Alyn. *On the right are the remains of Tomen-y-Faerdre – the 11thC fortress home of the Lords of Ial. The mound or 'motte' uses a natural rock outcrop and is ditched on the other sides. It originally supported a stone tower or 'bailey'. On the left is a large cave where prehistoric remains were found. The nearby farmhouse was once part of a medieval manor house. Continue to the B5430. Turn LEFT, then RIGHT, to follow the road towards Eryrys for ⅓ mile. Just beyond the Victorian primary school, take a way-marked path on the left along the access track to* Bryn Mywion.

2 When the track bends down left to the farm, go through a gate on your right. Now follow a faint track to go through a gateway ahead, then turn LEFT along another faint track. After about 100 yards, at an old field corner, turn RIGHT to pass between the boundary and a holly tree. Go through the field gap ahead then, go RIGHT into the small field behind a ruin. Head to the field end, over the old boundary, then swing LEFT to follow the boundary on the left, soon passing through trees to cross a stile in the wall ahead. Continue across the next field, over a stile ahead, and drop down to a lane. Go along the track opposite, passing a house, and at a track junction, swing half-LEFT up above a garage. *Here in the Nant, can be seen relics of the 19thC Great Westminster lead-mine – a chimney flue and the impressive engine house, which once contained a steam engine used to pump water from the mines. There was also a school here for miners' children.*

3 Just before a gate, turn LEFT on a rising enclosed path, soon passing Erw Nant. Follow its access track, over a cattle grid, and on down the left of two tracks. When it swings left by The Cottage, cross a stile on the right, and a wooden fence in the field corner. Now head half-LEFT alongside the boundary up through trees, soon reaching open ground with extensive views. Keep close to the wall to reach a small plateau – *a delightful limestone area of drystone walls, boulders and escarpment.* Cross a stile in the field corner, just below a transmitter mast, and continue ahead alongside the boundary on your right. After 50 yards swing half-LEFT to join a track that curves round the left-hand edge of the escarpment, passing near a lime kiln. Follow the track to pass through a gate.

4 Turn LEFT along an enclosed track (or right for refreshments at the Sun Inn in nearby Eryrys). After a few hundred yards, when the track begins to bend left, cross an old gate on the right, and a waymarked fence just ahead. Now head half-LEFT alongside the boundary on the left running beneath limestone crags. From the boundary corner, the path continues across open ground. When it swings down left, continue ahead on a fainter path passing two small trees, beneath a small rocky escarpment, and on along a part gorse-covered shelf – *providing*

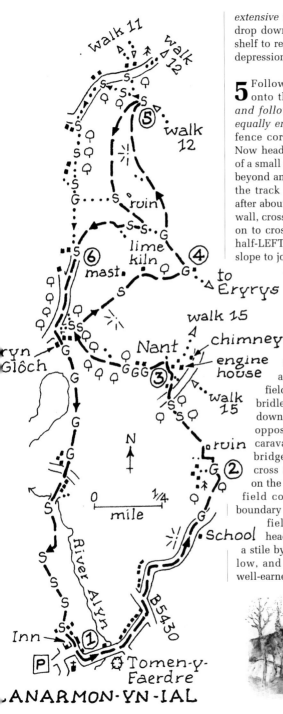

extensive views. After a few hundred yards, drop down half-LEFT on to the lower green shelf to reach a stile in the fence, in a small depression.

5 Follow the fence on the right back up onto the green shelf (*or cross the stile and follow the identified alternative, but equally enjoyable, route to point* **6**). At the fence corner go through an old gateway. Now head slightly LEFT, passing to the left of a small rocky knoll, before dropping down beyond an old boundary to cross a stile onto the track left earlier. Follow it LEFT and, after about 300 yards, by a jutting out corner wall, cross a stone stile on your right, and go on to cross a ladder-stile ahead. Now head half-LEFT over an old wall and on up the slope to join a delightful green track. Follow it RIGHT down to cross a stile by a house onto a lane.

6 Continue along the lane. Just beyond the access track to Fron Cottage, turn LEFT along a waymarked bridleway, passing in front of Bryn-y-Gloch and through a gate beyond. Continue down the field to follow the delightful enclosed bridleway along a quarry edge, and on down to a road. Take the enclosed path opposite, soon swinging RIGHT past a caravan site to cross a charming stone bridge over the river Alyn, and on to cross a stile. Now follow the boundary on the left round to cross a stile in the far field corner. Continue ahead with the boundary on your right, and across the next field to cross the stile ahead. Now head half-RIGHT up the field to cross a stile by the wall behind a modern bungalow, and on to reach the Raven Inn for a well-earned drink.

WALK 15
LIMESTONE AND LEAD

DESCRIPTION A 5¾ mile walk exploring the attractive limestone country south of Eryrys, visiting reminders of its lead-mining past, by linking together delightful short sections of paths and bridleway. Hundreds of men once worked in the mines which flourished in the area during periodic booms of the 18th and 19th centuries, but by the early 20thC the mines had closed. The route includes one of the best sections of open high-level limestone walking in the area, through a Site of Special Scientific Interest. Allow about 3 hours. The route can easily be shortened to a 4½ mile walk.

START Eryrys [SJ 204578].

DIRECTIONS Turn off the A494 Ruthin-Mold road on the B5430 towards Llanarmon-yn-ial. Soon take a road left to Eryrys then, at the Sun Inn, turn left into Caer Odyn, where there is road side parking on the right.

Eryrys was built in the early 19thC in response to expanding lead-mining operations in the area and, at its peak, the parish, including Graianrhyd, boasted a population of over 1000.

1 From the crossroads take the road towards Graianrhyd, and after a few hundred yards, take a waymarked path on the right. Follow the boundary on the right to cross a stile in the field corner. Turn LEFT up to cross another stile, then follow the boundary on the left through several fields to reach a track – *enjoying extensive views of Llantisilio Mountains, the Berwyns, the Arans and distant Snowdonia to the west.* Follow the track LEFT, soon passing Bog Isa and a pool. *Nearby is the site of Bog mine – once one of the area's biggest lead-mines. Between 1925-38 spar (used mainly for pebble-dashing houses) was extracted from its waste tips, and limestone removed.* At the top of a rise, keep with the left of three tracks to a road. Follow the road to the RIGHT.

2 Just before a house, turn RIGHT through a kissing gate on a waymarked bridleway, soon passing an old chimney flue, mine entrance and small pool. Continue with the delightful enclosed bridleway, dropping down to a road. Turn LEFT along the road to Graianrhyd. (*A shorter alternative to point 4 is to turn right, then just past Graig quarry, take a path on the left. Go half-right to follow a green track rising gently over open pasture, and on through a small wood to cross a stile by a house. Cross a gate in front, then continue ahead to follow a clear path through the trees and on with the boundary down to the road*). Just beyond a telephone box at Maes Gwyn estate, take a path on the right over a stile. Go along the field edge to cross a footbridge in the corner. Now go half-RIGHT across the next field, and on to cross a ladder-stile ahead. Go up the rise ahead and on to pass through a gate. Head half-RIGHT across a large field to reach the boundary fence of the house ahead. Follow it up through trees to cross a stile, then continue half-LEFT to drop down through a gate to a lane. Turn LEFT.

3 Almost immediately, turn RIGHT over a stile, and follow the boundary on your left through a wet area to cross a stile in the field corner. Now follow the bottom edge of the gorse-covered slopes of the next field round to cross a stile onto a lane. Follow it RIGHT to go through the entrance to 18thC Allt Gymbyd Farm and on between outbuildings to cross a stile ahead. Continue along the field edge to drop down onto a golf link (tee number 2) to cross a ladder-stile on the right. Continue ahead between delightful tree-covered limestone ridges and, at the end of the clearing, at a prominent waymark post on the rise ahead, turn RIGHT and, after a few yards, turn LEFT over a stile. Continue ahead by lorries, outbuildings and a house to a road.

4 Turn LEFT, then cross a waymarked ladder-stile set back on the left to follow a delightful enclosed path, featuring heavily mossed stones. At its end, cross a stile and continue down a narrow field to pass in front of a house, before swinging RIGHT down to

the road. Turn RIGHT. Then, shortly, turn LEFT up a track opposite a lane, and continue on with a path to cross a stile behind a house. Continue ahead alongside an old wall on your right on a delightful path rising steadily across the open limestone grassland of Graig – *a SSSI consisting of a series of stepped limestone ridges and pavements, offering panoramic views.* At the end of the wall, continue ahead, dropping gently down before rising up a wide green shelf beneath a limestone escarpment. You soon begin descending towards houses and a quarry, swinging LEFT down to a road. Follow it RIGHT up the hill.

5 Just before Castell Bach turn LEFT along a track. After merging with another track, follow a grey path below areas of 'silver sand' – *a waste product of lead-mining activity* – to drop down to a lane. Turn LEFT, then take a waymarked

GRAIANRHYD

path on the right. *Ahead are the remains of an impressive engine house that once contained a powerful steam engine used to pump water out of a mine in the Nant, and above is a chimney flue.* The path drops down to a cross-road of tracks. Here turn RIGHT towards a white house set just below the engine house. A large wooden gate at its rear right-hand side reveals a delightful enclosed path, which you follow up the narrow valley, passing a cottage, continuing up its access track, then a lane to a junction. Follow the lane RIGHT, back to the start, and perhaps a drink at the Sun Inn.

31

PRONUNCIATION

These basic points should help non-Welsh speakers

Welsh	English equivalent
c	always hard, as in cat
ch	as on the Scottish word loch
dd	as th in then
f	as v in vocal
ff	as f
g	always hard as in got
ll	no real equivalent. It is like 'th' in then, but with an 'L' sound added to it, giving 'thlan' for the pronunciation of the Welsh 'Llan'.

In Welsh the accent usually falls on the last-but-one syllable of a word.

KEY TO THE MAPS

- ➤ Walk route and direction
- Metalled road
- Unsurfaced road
- •••• Footpath/route adjoining walk route
- River/stream
- ⋏ ᗣ Trees
- ▬▬ Railway
- **G** Gate
- **S** Stile
- F.B. Footbridge
- Viewpoint
- P Parking
- T Telephone

THE COUNTRY CODE

Enjoy the countryside and respect its life and work

Guard against all risk of fire

Leave gates *as you find them*

Keep your dogs under close control

Keep to public paths across farmland

Use gates and stiles to cross fences, hedges and walls

Leave livestock, crops and machinery alone

Take your litter home

Help to keep all water clean

Protect wildlife, plants and trees

Take special care on country roads

Make no unnecessary noise

Published by
Kittiwake 3 Glantwymyn Village Workshops, nr Machynlleth, Montgomeryshire SY20 8LY

© Text and map research: David Berry 2000
© Maps & illustrations: Kittiwake 2000
Drawings by Morag Perrott

Cover photographs: David Berry – large: Limestone pavement (walk 15), inset: White Horse Inn, Cilcain (walks 7 & 9).

Care has been taken to be accurate. However neither the author nor the publisher can accept responsibility for any errors which may appear, or their consequences. If you are in doubt about any access, check before you proceed.

Printed by WPG, Welshpool, Powys.
First edition: 2000
Revised reprint: 2002

ISBN: **1 902302 10 9**